Luisenpark Mannheim

Neckar
Mannheim-City
D
Fernmeldeturm
5
Joseph - Braun - Ufer
Hans - Reschke - Ufer
E
Medicusstraße
Bassermannstraße
Parksee Kutzerweiher
Duo Jing-Bahn
Unterer Luisen-park
Ludwig - Ratzel - Straße
C
B
A
Kolpingstraße
62
Lanz-Villa
60
Erzbergerstraße
Otto Beck Straße
Am Oberen Luisenpark
Kutzerweiher
62
Am oberen Luisenpark
6 9 62
Planetarium
LUISENPARK
Alles im grünen Bereich!
Kunstobjekte im Park
Duo Jing-Bahn im Park
Stadtbahnlinie
Stadtbuslinie
0 50 100 m
© www.derplan-online.de 02/2009
DER PLAN
© www.derplan-online.de

Heidelberg
5 OEG
Josef-Bußjäger-Weg
Duo Jing-Bahn
Gartenschauweg
heodor-Heuss-Anlage
riedensplatz 1, 2, 3
Landesmuseum

Blick auf den Fernmeldeturm
View of the telecommunication tower

LIEBE LESER,

oder besser: Liebe Betrachter! Denn in Ihren Händen halten Sie ein Bilderbuch. Als solches jedenfalls hat der Feudenheimer Verlag Waldkirch dieses Buchprojekt mit über 160 stimmungs- und ausdrucksvollen Fotos vom Luisenpark, Mannheims beliebtester Freizeiteinrichtung, konzipiert und definiert. Gerne haben wir unsere Zustimmung zur Verwirklichung des Projektes gegeben und mit Spannung und Neugier das Ergebnis erwartet. Denn eines ist sicher: An kaum einem anderem Ort in Mannheim wird so oft und so viel fotografiert wie im Luisenpark. Damit würde es nicht leicht, uns mit neuen Perspektiven und fotografischen Interpretationen zu überraschen. Sicher war aber auch, dass mit Elsa Hennseler-Etté eine von uns hochgeschätzte Fotografin und Kennerin des Parks für die Bebilderung engagiert wurde.

So ganz ohne Text kommen auch die meisten Bilderbücher nicht aus. Gerade der Luisenpark nennt neben einer besonderen Historie, eine außergewöhnliche Tier- und Pflanzenwelt sowie ein vielfältiges Veranstaltungsprogramm sein eigen. Das ein oder andere Wörtchen darüber zu verlieren, ist also unabdingbar. Wir haben uns sehr gefreut, dass Peter W. Ragge sich bereit erklärt hat, die Texte für das Buch zu schreiben. Einen parkaffineren Schreiber hätte der Verlag kaum finden können als den gebürtigen Mannheimer und Vollblutjournalisten.

Nun liegt uns und Ihnen das Buch zum Luisenpark vor. Und das Konzept ist voll aufgegangen. Elsa Hennseler-Etté ist es tatsächlich gelungen, weitere, neue Park-Perspektiven und Stimmungen fotografisch festzuhalten. Bild- und Wortsprache drücken überzeugend aus, was dieses grüne Fleckchen mitten in der Stadt so liebenswert macht und welchen Beitrag es dazu leistet, Mannheim so lebenswert zu machen.

Sehen Sie selbst!

Herzlichst Ihr

DEAR READERS,

Or should I say: Dear viewers! Because in your hands you have a picture book. It was the intention of Feudenheim-based publishers Waldkirch to create a book of more than 160 atmospheric and expressive photos of the Luisenpark, Mannheim's most popular recreational destination. We were glad to support the realisation of the project and awaited the result with excitement and curiosity, because one thing is certain: practically nowhere else in Mannheim is photographed as much or as often as the Luisenpark. Therefore it was not easy to surprise us with new views and photographic interpretations. But we were also sure that in Elsa Hennseler-Etté, we had an esteemed photographer and connoisseur of the park.

Most picture books need at least some text. The Luisenpark has an unusual history and an exceptional range of plants and animals, not to mention a diverse programme of events. It was therefore essential to write a word or two about it. We were delighted that Peter W. Ragge agreed to compose the texts for the book. The publishers would have been hard-pressed to find an author with a greater affinity for the park than this Mannheim-born journalist.

We – and you – now have the book about the Luisenpark in our hands, and it is a complete success. Elsa Hennseler-Etté has really been able to capture new moods and views of the park with her camera. The images and words clearly express what makes this green space in the middle of the city so attractive, and how it helps to improve the quality of life in Mannheim.

Take a look for yourself!

Yours,

Joachim Költzsch

DER SOMMERTRAUM ENDET NIE

Er fuhr nicht „Hoch auf dem gelben Wagen" vor, wie er damals immer sang, aber er schipperte gerne in der Gondoletta, den kleinen Booten mit dem gelben Dach, durch den Luisenpark: Walter Scheel, der damalige Bundespräsident. 1975 kam er nach Mannheim, um die Bundesgartenschau zu eröffnen. Und jetzt, 35 Jahre später, weiß man, dass er mit seiner Ansprache völlig richtig lag: „Bei den Bundesgartenschauen geht es nicht nur darum, Blumen zu zeigen, sondern eine Stadt zu verschönern und Menschen, die auf engem Raum zusammenleben, den Zugang zur lebensspendenden Natur zu schaffen", sagte Scheel - und genau so ist es, denn das sommerlange Blütenfest wirkt noch Generationen später nach. 1,2 Millionen Menschen kommen nach wie vor Jahr für Jahr in den Luisenpark und machen ihn zur beliebtesten Freizeiteinrichtung der Region.

„Ein Fest verändert eine Stadt" hieß das Buch über den Sommer 1975 in der Quadratestadt - mit gutem Grund. Schließlich sind Mannheim nicht nur zwei herrliche, nach wie vor auch überregionale Besuchermassen anziehende Parks geblieben mit der Multihalle und der Seebühne, dem Fernmeldeturm und dem Pflanzenschauhaus. Die ganze Herzogenriedbebauung mit dem Gemeindezentrum und dem Jugendhaus, die Erweiterung des Rosengartens um den Mozartsaal, die Fußgängerzone in den Planken und vieles mehr wäre ohne die Bundesgartenschau undenkbar gewesen. Die Stadt, besonders

THE MIDSUMMER DREAM NEVER ENDS

Walter Scheel, the Federal German President of the day, didn't ride "High on the yellow carriage," as in the German folksong he always used to sing, but he did like to sail through the Luisenpark in a gondoletta, the small boat with the yellow roof. In 1975 he came to Mannheim to open the German Federal Garden Show, and today, 35 years on, we know how true his words back then were: "The purpose of the Federal Garden Shows is not just to show flowers, but to make a city more beautiful and give people who live together at close quarters access to life-giving nature," Scheel said – and he was right; we are still enjoying the summer-long pageant of petals and blossoms generations later. 1.2 million people continue to visit the Luisenpark year on year, making it one of the most popular recreational destinations in the region.

"Ein Fest verändert eine Stadt" [a festival changes a city] is the name of the book about the summer of 1975 in Mannheim – and with good reason. After all, Mannheim not only gained two magnificent parks that continue to attract visitors from near and far, with the Multihalle building and Seebühne stage on the lake, telecommunication tower and Plant House. The entire Herzogenried development with the community centre and youth centre, the Mozartsaal extension to the Rosengarten, the pedestrianised area in the Planken and much more would have been inconceivable without the Federal Garden Show. The city, then particularly stricken by the first

Fahnenhügel
Flags on the hill

gebeutelt von der damals gerade grassierenden ersten großen Wirtschaftskrise nach dem Krieg und dem Strukturwandel der Industrie, erlebte plötzlich eine ungeahnte Euphorie, einen Ruck, einen Aufschwung, wie er seither nie mehr zu spüren war.

Zwar gab es den Luisenpark bereits seit den Jahren 1892/1903, als er angelegt und 1896 nach der Großherzogin Luise von Baden, Tochter Kaiser Wilhelms I., benannt wurde. Aber er war nicht mehr als eben eine Grünanlage zum Sonntagsspaziergang. Zur - am Friedrichsplatz stattfindenden - „Internationalen Kunst- und Großen Gartenbau-Ausstellung" anlässlich der 300-Jahr-Feier der Stadt Mannheim 1907 hatte man eine Palmenhalle in Höhe der Werderstraße errichtet, die man danach - als Vorgänger des heutigen Pflanzenschauhauses - an den Luisenpark verlegte, erweiterte und 1909 als „Palmenhaus" der Öffentlichkeit übergab. Im Krieg zerstört, entstand dann 1958 das Pflanzenschauhaus.

Zur Bundesgartenschau kam ein Großteil der ehemaligen Rennwiese, die nach 1945 als Golfplatz genutzt wurde, dazu, wuchs die grüne Oase inmitten der Innenstadt auf heute 42 Hektar. Auch den zuvor arg heruntergekommenen Herzogenriedpark hat man 1975 um ein Wohngebiet und Kleingärten ergänzt, insgesamt 690 000 Kubikmeter Erde bewegt, 50 200 Quadratmeter neue Wasserflächen geschaffen, 557 Bäume gepflanzt, unzählige Blüten zum Blühen gebracht und 50 Millionen Mark ausgegeben, 1500 Veranstaltungen in 185 Tagen organisiert, enorm Werbung gemacht. Der Lohn: Schon vor der Eröffnung waren 150 000 Dauerkarten ver-

really serious economic crisis after the war and the structural changes in industry, suddenly experienced an undreamt-of euphoria, a jolt, an upturn the like of which has not been felt since.

The Luisenpark has been in existence since 1892/1903, when it was built, and 1896, when it was named after Grand Duchess Luise of Baden, daughter of Kaiser Wilhelm I, but it was no more than a green space for Sunday strolls. At the "International Art and Horticulture Exhibition" held on Friedrichsplatz to mark the 300-year anniversary of the city of Mannheim in 1907, a palm building was built on a level with Werderstraße, which – as a precursor to today's Plant House – was then moved to the Luisenpark, was extended and presented to the public in 1909 as the "Palm House". It was destroyed in the war, and the Plant House was built in 1958.

The Federal Garden Show took in a large part of the former racetrack, which was used after 1945 as a golf course, and the green haven in the city centre grew to the 42 hectares it measures today. In 1975, a residential area and allotments were also built on the previously very rundown Herzogenriedpark, 690,000 m^3 of earth were moved, 50,200 m^2 of water areas were created, 557 trees and countless flowers planted and 50 million marks spent, 1500 events were organised in 185 days and a huge promotional campaign was launched. The reward: even before the opening, 150,000 season tickets were sold, and 8.1 million visitors, 200,000 in the first three days alone, flocked to the Federal Garden Show – more than ever before, and a figure that has not been topped since.

kauft, allein in den ersten drei Tagen strömten 200 000 Besucher, insgesamt sogar 8,1 Millionen Besucher - so viele wie noch nie und nie mehr bei einer Bundesgartenschau.

In Mannheim ist die Erinnerung an das grandiose sommerlange Blütenfest nie verblasst. Die Bürger haben - ganz entgegen der Absicht der Stadtverwaltung - entschieden, dass die Zäune nach der Bundesgartenschau bleiben sollen, der Park weiter Eintritt verlangt und dafür auf hohem Niveau gepflegt wird. Und ein bisschen feiert man einfach immer weiter, bei Parkfesten, beim Lagerfeuer auf der Freizeitwiese oder beim kulturträchtigen „Seebühnenzauber". Ob mit Klangoase, Bauernhof, Pinguingehege, Kakteenhaus, tropischem Schmetterlingsparadies, Heilpflanzengarten oder 2001 mit einem chinesischen Garten sowie dem größten original chinesischen Teehaus auf dem europäischen Kontinent - der Park wird ständig weiter ergänzt, modernisiert.

Was er behält, ist das liebenswürdige Flair eines familiengerechten Naherholungsgebietes, das - durch den Zaun, striktes Hundeverbot und häufige Kontrollgänge - sechs herrliche, fantasiereiche und insbesondere stets saubere, abwechslungsreiche Spielplätze sowie eine riesige, 8000 Quadratmeter Rasen umfassende Freizeitwiese mit viel Raum zum Spielen bietet. Aber auch Schachecken, Minigolf, ein von Skulpturen gesäumter Spazierweg oder eine spezielle Behindertenschaukel gibt es. Ob Kinder laut umhertollen oder mit dem Spielzeugbagger im Matsch graben wollen, ob man einfach auf bequemen Liegen in stillen Winkeln entspannen

In Mannheim, the memory of the wonderful summer-long pageant of blossoms and petals has never faded. Citizens decided – contrary to the city administration's intentions – that the fences should stay put after the Federal Garden Show ended, and that an entrance fee should be charged to enable the park to be maintained to a high standard. And the celebrations there continue – in park festivals, campfires on the meadow or the cultural "Seebühnenzauber" [lake stage magic] events. The park is being constantly developed and modernised, for example with a "haven of sound", farmyard, penguin enclosure, cactus house, tropical butterfly house, medicinal herb garden or, in 2001, the Chinese Garden and the largest original Chinese teahouse on the European continent.

What it has retained is the attractive flair of a family-friendly recreational area that – thanks to the perimeter fence, a strict ban on dogs and frequent patrols – offers six magnificent, imaginative and, in particular, always clean, diverse playgrounds and a huge, 8000 m² meadow with plenty of room to play. But there are also chess corners, crazy golf, a walk lined with sculptures or a special swing for the disabled. A place for children to run around or play with toy diggers in the mud, a place to find a quiet corner to lie down and relax and or stroll along the babbling mountain stream – since 1975, Mannheim has been home to one of the most beautiful parks in Europe, a green haven for all generations, just a few minutes from the city centre.

und in völliger Ruhe am plätschernden Gebirgsbach entlang flanieren möchte - von 1975 blieb eine der schönsten Parkanlagen Europas, ein grünes Paradies für alle Generationen, und das nur wenige Minuten vom Stadtzentrum entfernt.

Peter W. Ragge

Der Jäger aus Kurpfalz

Er ist seit 1974 der bekannteste Botschafter und Sympathieträger des Luisenparks und ganz Mannheims: Fred Reibold, der „Jäger aus Kurpfalz". Und er ist ein Beispiel dafür, wie einem mit viel Mut, mitten im Schlamassel, der Neuanfang gelingen kann. Aus der Arbeitslosigkeit heraus wurde er von einer der Mitarbeiterinnen der ersten Stunde der Bundesgartenschau 1975 entdeckt Er nahm Reitstunden, übte im Wald Hornsignale und wurde so das Maskottchen der Bundesgartenschau, absolvierte Werbeeinsätze in der ganzen Bundesrepublik. Unzählige kleine Kinder machte er glücklich, als er sie auf seinem Ross mitreiten ließ. Tausende von Erinnerungsfotos entstanden mit ihm. Mit seinem liebevoll-herzlichen Charme machte er sich so viele Freunde, dass er auch nach Ende des sommerlangen Fests für einige Auftritte im Jahr verpflichtet wurde. Unermüdlich ist er weiter für die grünen Oasen unterwegs. 400 Schlager und 40 Jagdsignale - das ist sein Repertoire. Ob Maimarkt oder Parkfeste - ohne sein Hornsignal würde eben einfach etwas fehlen.

Vicco von Bülow alias Loriot zeichnete den „Jäger aus Kurpfalz", mit der typischen Knollennase und auf einer Flinte reitend, als witzige Karikatur, die seit der Bundesgartenschau lange Jahre für den Park Werbung gemacht hat.

Alte Aufnahme aus dem Gartenschaujahr 1975
Old photograph taken at the Federal Garden Show 1975

The huntsman from Kurpfalz

Since 1974, he has been the most famous ambassador and a popular figure in the Luisenpark and the whole of Mannheim: Fred Reibold, the "huntsman from Kurpfalz". He is one example of how, with great courage, someone can overcome adversity and make a new start. At the time unemployed, he was discovered by one of the Federal Garden Show's first employees in 1975. He took riding lessons, practiced bugle calls in the forest, and became the mascot of the Garden Show, going on promotional campaigns across the Federal Republic. He made countless children happy by letting them ride on his horse, and thousands of memories were captured in photos with him. With his warm and charming manner, he made so many friends that even when the summer's festivities were over, he was still commissioned to appear a couple of times in the year. He is still a tireless campaigner for the green haven. His repertoire comprises 400 hits and 40 bugle calls. Without his bugle calls, something would be missing – be it at the Maimarkt or festivals at the park.

Vicco von Bülow, also known as Loriot, drew the "huntsman from Kurpfalz" with the typical bulbous nose and riding a musket, as a humorous caricature, which has been used to promote the park for many years since the Federal Garden Show.

Päonienblüte
Peony

Fernmeldeturm

Von hier oben sieht man, in welch herrliche Landschaft Mannheim eingebettet und wie sehr die Stadt von Grünflächen durchzogen ist. Der Fernmeldeturm wurde - mit 64 Pfählen elf Meter tief im Erdreich verankert - von 1973 an errichtet und zur Bundesgartenschau 1975 eröffnet. Das zunächst 205, nach Installation einer neuen Antenne dann 212 Meter messende höchste Gebäude der Stadt hatte zu Anfang eine sehr wichtige Funktion als Antennenträger für die damalige Bundespost (später Telekom), die hier mehrere Richtfunkstrecken für Telefon und Datendienste bündelte. Doch seit immer mehr Glasfaserkabel verlegt werden, hat der Turm diese Funktion weitgehend verloren.

Zwei Aufzüge bringen - mit einer Geschwindigkeit von sechs Metern pro Sekunde - Besucher auf ein Aussichtsgeschoss mit Bistro in 121 Metern Höhe oder ins Drehrestaurant „Skyline“ in 125 Metern Höhe. Das dreht sich einmal in der Stunde um die eigene Achse - man kann also speisen und den Rundblick in die ganze Region genießen oder aus luftiger Höhe nochmal seinen Spaziergang durch den Luisenpark nachvollziehen.

Telecommunication tower

From up here, you have a really excellent view of the superb landscape in which Mannheim is situated and the large number of green areas all around the city. Construction of the telecommunication tower, with 64 piles driven 11 metres into the ground, started in 1973 and the building was opened at the Federal Garden Show in 1975. The highest building in the city, initially measuring 205 metres but extending to 212 metres after the installation of a new antenna, originally had an extremely important function as an antenna tower for the then Bundespost (later Telekom), which consolidated several radio links for telephony and data services here. However, as more and more fibre optic cables were laid, the tower has largely lost this function.

Two elevators, travelling at a speed of six metres per second, bring visitors to a viewing level with a bistro at a height of 121 metres, or the "Skyline" rotating restaurant at 125 metres. It completes a full rotation around its own axis once an hour, allowing you to enjoy a panoramic view of the entire region, or retrace the steps of your walk through the Luisenpark, while you dine.

Ein blühender Kaiser Barbarossa - speziell angelegt zum Stauferjahr 2010
Frederick Barbarossa in bloom – created specially to mark the Hohenstaufen Year 2010

Der Kutzerweiher von oben aus dem Drehrestaurant
The Kutzer Lake from above - out of the rotating restaurant

DREHRESTAURANT SKYLINE

Speisen in luftigen 125 Metern Höhe, ein Blick vom Odenwald bis zur Haardt - das Drehrestaurant ist der richtige Ort, um sich in entspannter Atmosphäre einen Überblick über Mannheim und die angrenzende Rheinebene zu verschaffen, und sich danach z.B. in den Trubel des Shoppings in Mannheims Einkaufsmeile zu stürzen, den herrlichen Luisenpark zu erkunden oder einen Wohlfühlabend im Abendrot zu starten.

Ab 10 Uhr morgens bringen die beiden Lifte Gäste auf das Rund der Restaurant-Plattform. Die gepflegte Karte, deutsch und französisch, mit saisonalen Schmankerln, bietet Abwechslung für Groß und Klein. In der Wein- und Getränkekarte findet sich die ergänzende Abrundung des Geschmackserlebnisses mit ausgesuchten Weinen der Region und einem kleinen französischen Schwerpunkt.

Egal welchen der 180 Plätze man sich aussucht, innerhalb einer Stunde wechselt ständig die Perspektive, denn das Restaurant dreht sich unmerklich um die Turmachse.

In diesem Wahrzeichen Mannheims ist gut sein, ob man Gäste von außerhalb bewirten und ihnen dabei Mannheims Topografie erläutern möchte, einen persönlichen Anlass feiert oder sich einfach selbst etwas Gutes tun will. Und das Beste ist: Mit einem Gutschein kann man dieses beeindruckende Erlebnis sogar verschenken.

Freundlicher, zuvorkommender Service ist Firmenphilosophie. Küchenmeister Holger Polomski und seine Frau Roselyne, eine bezaubernde Französin aus Paris, halten die Fäden in der Hand. Unterstützt werden sie in der Küche von Sohn Florian, der nach einer Ausbildung zum Koch im Dorint-Hotel Mannheim und drei Jahren Erfahrung in den besten Häusern in Spanien, der Schweiz und der deutschen Sterneküche nun wieder zurück in den heimatlichen Gefilden ist.

DREHRESTAURANT SKYLINE

Dine at an airy height of 125 metres with a view from the Odenwald to the Haardt – the rotating restaurant is the ideal place to take in the scenery across Mannheim and the Rhine plane in a relaxed atmosphere; afterwards why not go on a shopping spree in Mannheim's shops, discover the magnificent Luisenpark or enjoy a cosy evening watching the sun go down?

From 10 in the morning, the two lifts transport guests to the restaurant platform. The exquisite menu featuring German and French cuisine with seasonal specialities offers a wide variety of choice for all. The wine list and drinks menu round off the taste experience, with selected wines from the region and from France.

Regardless of which of the 180 seats you choose, your view will constantly change over the hour as the restaurant rotates imperceptibly around the tower axis.

This landmark of Mannheim is the place to be, whether you want to dine out with guests who are unfamiliar with the city and want to show them Mannheim's landscape, you are celebrating something special or simply want to treat yourself. The best thing: With a voucher, you can even give this impressive experience as a gift.

Friendly, helpful service is the company's philosophy. Head chef Holger Polomski and his wife Roselyne, a charming Frenchwoman from Paris, are at the helm. They are assisted in the kitchen by son Florian, who is back on home ground after training to become a chef at the Dorint Hotel in Mannheim and three years' experience in the best restaurants in Spain and Switzerland as well as time in starred restaurants in Germany.

Hans-Reschke-Ufer 2 · 68165 Mannheim
Tel. (0621) 4 19 29-0 · info@skyline-ma.de
www.skyline-ma.de

GRÜNE VITRINEN

Ein wenig erinnert es an die Sammlervitrinen vergangener Jahrhunderte – das Pflanzenschauhaus mit seinen Anbauten. Unter dem schützenden Glas findet sich eine Vielzahl von Kostbarkeiten aus Fauna und Flora aus allen Kontinenten, die sich den staunenden Besucheraugen präsentieren.

GREEN SHOWCASES

The Plant House and its extensions are a little like the collectors' showcases of centuries gone by. Beneath the protective glass, amazed visitors find a myriad of fauna and flora treasures from every continent.

Pflanzenschauhaus
Plant House

Pflanzenschauhaus

Das Pflanzenschauhaus ist seit 1958 der Ersatz für das im Zweiten Weltkrieg zerstörte historische Palmenhaus. Es birgt die üppige Flora der Subtropen und Tropen. Mit mehr als 350 verschiedenen Pflanzenarten gestaltet sich ein Urwald im Kleinen, Abbild der heute so sehr bedrohten Urwälder, bevölkert von seltenen Tieren aus Afrika, Asien und Amerika.

Im geheimnisvollen Halbdunkel der Aquarien sind 350 verschiedene Fischarten versammelt und mehr als 50 verschiedene Reptilienarten haben in Terrarien das ihnen genehme Lebensumfeld gefunden.

Stachlige Gesellen zeigen sich im Kakteenhaus von ihrer attraktivsten Seite. Vor dem gewaltigen „Schwiegermuttersitz" (echinocactus grusonii) hat schon mancher Besucher sinnend verweilt.

Plant House

Since 1958, the Plant House has been the replacement for the historic Palm House destroyed in the Second World War. It houses the lush flora of the subtropics and tropics. With more than 350 different species of plant, it creates a mini-rainforest, a mirror of today's so endangered rainforests, inhabited by rare animals from Africa, Asia and America.

The mysterious semi-darkness of the aquariums is home to 350 different species of fish, and more than 50 different species of reptile have found their ideal environment in the terrariums.

Pricklier cohorts show off their best side in the Cactus House. Many a visitor has had pause for thought in front of the huge "mother-in-law's cushion" (echinocactus grusonii).

Liegewiese und Pflanzenschauhaus
Meadow and Plant House

Anakonda
Anaconda

„Schwiegermuttersitz"
"Mother-in-law's cushion"

Baumfarnhaus

Kühl und feucht geht es zu im Baumfarnhaus. Das neueste Gebäude im Pflanzenschauhaus-Ensemble zeigt die mächtigen lebenden Fossilien in ihrer (beinahe) natürlichen Umgebung. Ursprünglich in den Regenwäldern Südamerikas, Südafrikas, Australiens, Neuseelands oder Malaysias beheimatet, haben die Baumfarne, die in ihrer Form irgendwie Palmen ähneln, hier im Herzen der Metropolregion Rhein-Neckar Wurzeln geschlagen, sehr zur Freude der Tausenden von Besuchern, die sie bewundern.

Das Baumfarnhaus wurde maßgeblich mit Spenden vom Förderkreis „Freunde des Luisenparks e.V." errichtet.

Tree Fern House

The Tree Fern House is cool and damp. The most recent of the Plant House buildings shows these huge living fossils in their (almost) natural environment. Originally native to the rainforests of South America, South Africa, Australia, New Zealand or Malaysia, the tree ferns, whose form is somehow similar to that of palm trees, have put down roots in the heart of the Rhine-Neckar region, much to the delight of thousands of admiring visitors.

The Tree Fern House was primarily built with donations by the association „Freunde des Luisenparks e.V." [Friends of the Luisenpark].

Eröffnung des Baumfarnhauses am 8.5.2009
Opening of the Tree Fern House on May 8, 2009

Versteinerte „Saurier der Pflanzenwelt"
Fossilised "dinosaurs of the plant world"

Schmetterlingshaus

Seit 1996 flattert und schwirrt es im Schmetterlingshaus. Die ganze Vielfalt bunter Falter im tropischen Ambiente lässt sich in allen Entwicklungsschritten vom Ei bis zum schlüpfenden Schmetterling beobachten. Tafeln und Schaukästen am Eingang des Hauses sorgen für umfassende Informationen rund um das Leben der prachtvollen Flatterwesen.

Butterfly House

The Butterfly House has been a flutter of activity since 1996. In tropical surroundings, you can watch a whole range of colourful creatures in every stage of development, from egg to emerging butterfly. Boards and display boxes at the entrance provide detailed information about the lives of these fascinating insects.

Päonienblüte im Chinesischen Garten
Peony in the Chinese Garden

TEEHAUS

Mitten im 2001 angelegten chinesischen Garten liegt das größte original chinesische Teehaus Europas. An Ort und Stelle vom chinesischen Garten- und Landschaftsarchitekten Professor Li Zheng nach den Grundsätzen des Feng Shui, der chinesischen Wissenschaft von Wind und Wasser geplant, wurde diese Anlage im typischen südchinesischen Stil errichtet. Schlichte Naturmaterialien wie Naturstein, lackiertes Holz, Ziegeln und Fliesen gewährleisten höchstmögliche Authentizität.

Das Haus hat zwei Stockwerke, die häufig und gerne für Veranstaltungen und Teezeremonien genutzt werden,

Im Restaurant im Erdgeschoss und im beschaulichen Innenhof kann man unterschiedlichste chinesische Teesorten und kleine Leckereien genießen.

TEEHAUS

The largest original teahouse in Europe is located in the middle of the Chinese Garden, which was built in 2001. These grounds were built in the typical southern Chinese style, designed by the Chinese landscape architect Professor Li Zheng according to the principles of feng shui, the Chinese science of wind and water. Simple natural materials such as natural stone, lacquered wood, bricks and tiles ensure maximum authenticity.

The house has two storeys, which are popular for events and tea ceremonies.

In the ground-floor restaurant and the tranquil courtyard, you can sample a wide variety of Chinese teas and delicious treats.

Brücke und Eingang zum Teehaus und zum Chinesischen Garten

Bridge and entrance to the Teahouse and Chinese Garden

Der Garten der vielen Ansichten (chin. Duojingyuan) mit dem chinesischen Teehaus wurde in Zusammenarbeit mit Mannheims chinesischer Partnerstadt Zhenjiang, der Klaus-Tschira-Stiftung in Heidelberg und dem Ostasieninstitut Ludwigshafen angelegt. Grundstock für den Bau war das Vermächtnis von Diplom-Kaufmann Georg Schmuck.

Bei der Anlage des Gartens kam es Professor Li Zheng besonders auf die Harmonie der sieben Dinge an: Erde, Himmel, Steine, Wasser, Gebäude, Wege und Pflanzen müssen sich im Einklang befinden, Vorhandenes ist mit einzubeziehen, sodass im Ergebnis die Natur eine künstlerische Vollendung erfährt.

The Garden of Many Views (Chinese = Duojingyuan) containing the Chinese Teahouse was built in cooperation with Mannheim's twin town in China, Zhenjiang, the Klaus Tschira Foundation in Heidelberg and the East Asia Institute, Ludwigshafen. The bequest made by Georg Schmuck served as the basis for the building.

When designing the garden, Professor Li Zheng particularly focused on the harmony of the seven things: earth, air, stones, water, buildings, paths and plants must be in harmony, things that already exist must be incorporated so that the result is the artistic perfection of nature.

Schneebedeckter Innenhof
Snow-covered inner courtyard

WASSER IM PARK

Wasser ist ein prägendes Element im Park. Als Quelle, als Bachlauf, in Brunnen, im Weiher, auf den Wasserspielplätzen, als Wasserfall im chinesischen Garten - das belebende Nass ist in vielerlei Form vorhanden und Mensch, Tier und Pflanze von Nutzen.

WATER IN THE PARK

Water is a defining feature of the park. It is present in many forms - as a spring, stream, fountains, the lake, in the water playgrounds, as a waterfall in the Chinese Garden - and benefits people, animals and plants.

Kutzerweiher
Kutzer Lake

Kutzerweiher

Die größte zusammenhängende Wasserfläche im Park ist der Kutzerweiher, benannt nach dem ehemaligen Mannheimer Oberbürgermeister Theodor Kutzer. In seiner Form bildet er auf 40.000 Quadratmeter einen verschwundenen Neckararm nach. Auf ihm gleiten die Markenzeichen des Luisenparks dahin, die gelbbedachten Gondolettas, die sich mittels Seilzug auf einem Rundkurs von 1840 Metern bewegen. An zwei „Haltestellen" kann man aus- und zusteigen.

Allerlei Getier lebt im, auf und an den Ufern des Weihers. Riesige Karpfen schwimmen bettelnd neben den Kähnen dahin, immer in der Hoffnung auf einen Keks oder sonst etwas Essbares von oben. Ganze Entenfamilien und anderes Wildgeflügel bevölkern die Wasseroberfläche. Auf den großen Steinen sonnen sich Kormorane und Wasserschildkröten in den wärmenden Sonnenstrahlen.

Kutzer Lake

The largest cohesive body of water in the park is the Kutzer Lake, named after the former Mannheim mayor Theodor Kutzer. Over 40,000 m^2 its form echoes a branch of the Neckar that has since vanished. It's here we see the signature feature of the Luisenpark, the yellow-roofed gondolettas, which travel a 1840 metres circuit pulled on a cable. You can get on and off at two "stops".

All manner of animals live on and around the banks of the lake. Huge carp swim alongside the boats, always hoping for a biscuit or another titbit from above. Entire families of ducks and other wildfowl populate the surface of the water. On the large stones, cormorants and terrapins bask in the warm rays of the sun.

Anlegestelle am Fernmeldeturm
Landing stage at the telecommunication tower

Bachlauf

Einem Gebirgsbach nachgebildet, ist der Bachlauf eine Zone der Entspannung. Das Wasser sucht sich murmelnd seinen Weg um und über die großen Steine, die sich ihm in den Weg stellen. Brücken queren seinen Lauf und bieten interessante Aus- und Einblicke auf das strömende Element. An seinen Ufern findet man die typische Vegetation mit Bäumen, Sträuchern und Stauden. Die großen Wurzeln der Bäume bilden ein interessantes Geflecht, das, mit Moosen überzogen, an Beschreibungen aus dem Märchen erinnert.

Stream

The stream, which emulates a mountain stream, is a place of relaxation. The water babbles its way around and over the large stones in its path. Bridges cross its path and offer interesting views of the flowing water. Its banks contain typical vegetation with trees, shrubs and bushes. The large roots of the trees create a tangled mesh, which – encased in moss – recalls scenes from fairy tales.

Sensarium - Training für die Sinne
Sensarium - training for the senses

Skulpturen von Georg Ott, Mudau-Langenelz
Sculptures by Georg Ott, Mudau-Langenelz

Pilzausstellung im Pflanzenschauhaus
Fungi exhibition in the Plant House

Brunnen

Brunnen haben im Park die unterschiedlichsten Formen. Das kostbare Nass hüpft über „Tanzende Steine"(Christian Tobin, Heinrich-Vetter-Stiftung), braust in Fontänen über blütenschalenförmige Becken, dient der „Haarwaschenden" (Martin Mayer, Heinrich-Vetter-Stiftung) als Bassin und als kühlende Mitte unter filigranem Pavillon. Üoerall begegnen dem Spazierenden faszinierende Formen, in denen Wasser still ruht, lebendig sprüht und braust, sich von Kanten und Kübeln ergießt.

Fountains

The fountains in the park take a wide variety of forms. Water jumps over "Dancing Stones" (Christian Tobin, Heinrich Vetter Foundation), gushes over petal-shaped bowls, serves as a pool for the "Hair Washer" (Martin Mayer, Heinrich Vetter Foundation) and as a cooling centre below an ornate pavilion. Everywhere, walkers encounter fascinating forms in which water rests peacefully, dances with life, gushes over ledges and out of vessels.

Tanzende Steine
Dancing Stones

„Haarwaschende", Brunnenfigur von Martin Mayer neben der KlangOase. (Heinrich-Vetter-Stiftung)

"Hair washer", fountain sculpture by Martin Mayer in the KlangOase (Heinrich Vetter Foundation)

Wasserspielplatz

Von allen Anlagen sind für Kinder die Wasserspielplätze die attraktivsten. Wasser, Sonne, und als Höhepunkt noch etwas Sand - wozu in die Ferne schweifen, wenn man in allernächster Stadtnähe so toll spielen kann?

Water playgrounds

Of all the attractions at the park, the water playgrounds are the most popular among children. Water, sun, not to mention a bit of sand – why travel afar, when there's so much to be had on one's doorstep?

Bunte Wasserräder auf dem Wasserspielplatz
Colourful waterwheels at the water playground

Zwei Möglichkeiten von vielen zum Spielen und Entspannen- Minigolf und Riesenschach

Two of the many ways to relax and play – crazy golf and giant chess

SEEBÜHNENZAUBER

Seine Berufsbezeichnung: „Popforscher" - denn so heißt die gleichnamige Band, deren Kopf und Sänger Peter Baltruschat ist. Vor fünf Jahren initiierte der stets vor Ideen sprühende Impresario den „Seebühnenzauber". Der Stadtpark hat den musikalischen Leiter des Musik-Kabaretts Schatzkistl und Impresario vom Kulturnetz Mannheim Rhein-Neckar damit beauftragt, weil der bestens vernetzte Künstler und Kulturunternehmer die großen Stars wie die regionalen Größen in den Luisenpark holen kann.

LAKESIDE MAGIC

"Popforscher" is a German band fronted by singer Peter Baltruschat, and the band's name, which means "pop researcher", is in effect his job description. Five years ago, the ever-inventive impresario initiated "Seebühnenzauber" [lake stage magic]. The city park commissioned the musical director of the music cabaret "Schatzkistl" and head of the Mannheim/Rhine-Neckar cultural network because the well-connected artist and cultural entrepreneur is able to attract major stars and big local names to the Luisenpark.

Peter Baltruschat

Bei der 2005 ins Leben gerufenen Veranstaltungsreihe „Seebühnenzauber" verzaubert die Natur das Publikum wie auch die auftretenden Künstler. Die schon zur Bundesgartenschau 1975 errichtete, wie ein Amphitheater am Ufer des Kutzerweihers gelegene Seebühne liegt mitten im Grünen.

Enten schnattern, manchmal steckt ein Karpfen seinen Kopf aus dem Wasser, Störche fliegen über die Köpfe des Publikums hinweg - eine einzigartige, traumhafte Kulisse für wunderschöne Abende.

Rund 1000 Gäste können hier auf emporsteigenden, teilweise überdachten Zuschauerrängen und damit bei optimaler Sicht Klassik, Jazz, Rock und Pop, Kabarett und Comedy, Musicals und Ballett genießen. Viele Stars wie Milva, Juliette Gréco, Johnny Logan, Dionne Warwick, Marla Glen, Peter Kraus, Xavier Naidoo sowie der französische Jazzpianist Jacques Loussier sind hier schon, begeistert von der einmalig-romantischen Atmosphäre, gerne aufgetreten und haben ihr Publikum verzaubert.

In the "Seebühnenzauber" events, which began 2005, nature inspires both the audience and the artists. The stage, designed like an amphitheatre and located on the bank of the Kutzer Lake, was built for the Federal Garden Show in 1975 and is surrounded by greenery.

Ducks quack, now and again a carp pokes its head out of the water, storks fly over the audience's heads – a unique, fantastic backdrop for a wonderful evening.

Around 1,000 guests can enjoy classical music, jazz, musicals and ballet in the sloped, partially covered spectator area that affords a perfect view.

Many stars such as Milva, Juliette Greco, Johnny Logan, Xavier Naidoo, Dionne Warwick, Marla Glen and French jazz pianist Jacques Loussier have played here, inspired by the uniquely romantic atmosphere, and have captivated their audience.

Einzigartige Atmosphäre: Seebühne im Lichterzauber
Unique atmosphere: The Seebühne illuminated

„Der Hammer!" sagt Bülent Ceylan. Er kommt viel `rum, aber nirgendwo sonst „headbangen sogar Enten und Fische mit". Damit beschreibt der Star-Comedian das besondere Ambiente dieser Open Air-Bühne.

"Amazing!" says German comedian Bülent Ceylan. He gets about, but nowhere else has he seen "ducks and fish head-banging along". For him, the atmosphere at this open-air stage is something very special.

Bülent Ceylan

2 Mann und Xavier Naidoo

STEINWAY & SONS

Jacques Loussier

Marla Glen

Auto Auto

Christian „Chako“ Habekost

Winterschlaf
Winter sleep

Baumhain

Wenn das Wetter mal nicht mitspielt, ist der Oktogon der Festhalle Baumhain der „Schirm", der die Zuschauer auch bei Regen die Veranstaltung genießen lässt. Abgesehen von solchen Ausweichfunktionen ist der Baumhain ein beliebter Veranstaltungsort für Abibälle, Konzerte, Aufführungen und für Festlichkeiten aller Art – sommers wie winters, auch im privaten Rahmen.

Baumhain

If the weather doesn't cooperate, the octagon of the Baumhain festival hall acts as an "umbrella", enabling guests to enjoy the event even on a rainy day. In addition to providing an alternative in such circumstances, Baumhain is a popular venue for school-leaver balls, concerts, performances and for festivities and celebrations of all kinds – summer and winter, public and private.

KLEINODIEN

Kleinodien - Kostbarkeiten hat der Park viele zu bieten. Zu den Schönsten gehört der Citrus-Garten, aber auch der Heilpflanzengarten oder der kleine, aber feine Weinberg am Freizeithaus.

Die KlangOase ist eine Mannheim-spezifische Besonderheit, ebenso wie der Heinrich-Vetter-Weg, Kunstwerke, die mit der Natur eine Symbiose eingehen, mit ihr verschmelzen, sie betonen oder einen unverwechselbaren, ganz eigenen Akzent setzen.

LITTLE GEMS

The park has some lovely little gems, such as the citrus garden, medicinal herb garden or the small but exquisite vineyard at the Freizeithaus recreational centre.

The KlangOase ["haven of sound"] is unique to Mannheim, as is the Heinrich-Vetter-Weg, which contains artworks that interact and merge with nature, accentuate it or make their own, quite distinctive mark.

Der Sonnengott, Beschützer von Flora und Fauna von Laszlo Szabo (Heinrich-Vetter-Stiftung)

The Sun God, Protector of Flora and Fauna by Laszlo Szabo (Heinrich Vetter Foundation)

Citrusgarten

Zu den Besonderheiten im Park gehört ohne Zweifel der Citrusgarten. Mit seinen mediterranen Elementen wie Postamenten, Holzbänkchen und Mauern aus gelbem Lava-Tuffstein, überspannt von einem filigranen Eisenpavillon, zaubert er Urlaubsstimmung mitten in Mannheim. 150 Pflanzenarten aus dem Süden wachsen hier. Darunter finden sich so unbekannte Spezies wie Bergamotten, Pomeranzen, Tangelos, Calamondin und viele mehr, aber auch unsere sattsam bekannten Zitronen, Orangen, Satsumas und Clementinen. Toskana-Feeling einfach beim Reinschnuppern.

Citrus garden

One of the real highlights in the park is undoubtedly the citrus garden. With its Mediterranean elements such as pedestals, wooden benches and walls of yellow volcanic tuff, spanned by an ornate iron pavilion, it provides a holiday atmosphere in the middle of Mannheim. 150 species of plant from the south are on display here, including such unfamiliar species as bergamots, bitter oranges, ugli, calamondin and many more, as well as our familiar lemons, oranges, satsumas and clementines. You are practically transported to Tuscany the moment you walk in.

KlangOase

Nur liegen und lauschen - für viele Besucher des Luisenparks gibt es keine erholsamere Stelle als die KlangOase. In dem von Büschen umgebenen Areal unweit des Fernmeldeturms ertönt harmonisch-romantische, mal melancholische, mal stimulierende Instrumentalmusik, speziell für den Luisenpark komponiert von dem bekannten Synthesizer-Virtuosen und Mannheimer Komponisten Peter Seiler, kombiniert mit Klangbildern aus der Natur wie Vogelgezwitscher, Grillenzirpen, Donnergrollen oder Plätschern des Wassers. Vier CDs hat er dazu schon eingespielt. Stets zwischen Mai und Oktober, von 9 Uhr bis zum Einbruch der Dämmerung, werden die sechs Lautsprecherboxen hoch droben in den Kronen von Schwarznuss, Baumhasel und Esche eingeschaltet. Es sind elektronisch erzeugte Klänge, vermischt mit traditionellen Orchesterinstrumenten, unglaublich melodisch, beruhigend, faszinierend - gerade im Zusammenspiel mit der Natur, denn zur Musik kommt das Rauschen der Blätter, das Schnattern der Enten aus dem Kutzerweiher, das Zwitschern der Vögel. Dazu kann man sich in Liegestühlen fernab des Besucherstroms völlig entspannen, manchmal saust sogar ein gar nicht scheues Eichhörnchen vorbei.

Riesenohr-Skulptur des Bildhauers Rolf Hook

Giant Ear sculpture by Rolf Hook

KlangOase

Simply lie back and listen – for many visitors to the Luisenpark, there's nowhere more relaxing than the KlangOase ["haven of sound"]. In the grounds enclosed by bushes, not far from the telecommunication tower, harmonious, romantic, sometimes melancholy, sometimes stimulating instrumental music plays, composed specially by the well-known synthesizer virtuoso and Mannheim composer Peter Seiler and combined with sounds from nature such as birdsong, cricket chirping, rolls of thunder or the splashing of water. He has already recorded four CDs of this music. Between May and October, from nine in the morning until dusk, the six loudspeakers high up in the canopies of the black walnut, Turkish hazel and ash are switched on. Electrical sounds are combined with traditional orchestral instruments, wonderfully melodic, calming, fascinating – particularly in combination with nature, as the music is complemented by the rustle of leaves, quacking of ducks on the Kutzer Lake and the chirruping of birds. Far away from the bustle of visitors, you can completely relax in a recliner, and occasionally, an undaunted squirrel might even hop by.

Heinrich-Vetter-Weg

Er ist wie ein modernes Museum im Freien: der Heinrich-Vetter-Weg. Ein herrlich erholsamer, schattiger Spazierweg unter hohen, alten, weit ausladenden Bäumen. Zwischen all dem Grün blitzt dann und wann chrom-glänzender Stahl hervor, sieht man geheimnisvoll anmutende Gebilde aus Granit, Eisen, Bronze, Messing oder Marmor. Manche, so scheint es, stehen schon ewig hier und sind Teil der Natur geworden, andere provozieren bewusst. Initiiert hat den ab 1992 angelegten Weg, der gegenüber dem Pflanzenschauhaus beginnt und sich auf der Wiese bis zum Burgspielplatz erstreckt, der 2003 verstorbene großherzige Mannheimer Mäzen und Ehrenbürger Heinrich Vetter.

Ein eigens von Professor Anton Eberwein geschaffenes Kunstwerk „Arbor Arborum" (Der Baum der Bäume) vollendet den Heinrich-Vetter-Weg seit 2009.

Nicht nur auf dem Heinrich-Vetter-Weg, sondern auch an anderen Plätzen im Park sind insgesamt 27 Skulpturen und Plastiken berühmter Künstler aus dem In- und Ausland zu sehen.

Heinrich-Vetter-Weg

The Heinrich-Vetter-Weg is like a modern, open-air museum. A wonderfully relaxing, shaded walkway under tall, old, expansive trees. Among all this green, gleaming steel emerges here and there, and you perceive mysterious forms in granite, iron, bronze, brass or marble. Some, so it would seem, have been here forever and have become one with nature, others intentionally provoke. The generous Mannheim patron and honorary citizen Heinrich Vetter, who died in 2003, initiated the route, the creation of which began in 1992, and which starts opposite the Plant House and continues along the meadow to the castle playground. Since 2009, the work "Arbor Arborum" (the tree of trees), specially created by Professor Anton Eberwein, has completed the Heinrich-Vetter-Weg.

A total of 27 sculptures by famous artists from Germany and abroad can be found not just along the Heinrich-Vetter-Weg, but also at other points in the park.

HEINRICH-VETTER-WEG

Ungewöhnliche Perspektive: Zwei Steinhörner (Anna Maria und Wolfgang Kubach-Wilmsen

Unusual perspectives: Two stone horns (Anna Maria and Wolfgang Kubach-Wilmsen)

„Neugier" (hinten) und „Zeitklammer" (vorne) von Erich Sauer

"Neugier" [curiosity] (back) and "Zeitklammer" [time bracket] (front) by Erich Sauer

„Apus" von Hartmut Stielow
"Apus" by Hartmut Stielow

„Raumfaltung I und Raumfaltung II“ von Ben Muthofer

“Raumfaltung I und Raumfaltung II” [folded space I and II] by Ben Muthofer

Arbum Arborum, der „Baum der Bäume"von Anton Eberwein
Arbum Arborum, the "tree of trees", by Anton Eberwein

„Baum der Eitelkeit" von Hans-Michael Kissel
"Baum der Eitelkeit" [tree of vanity] by Hans-Michael Kissel

„Bündelung" von Alf Lechner
"Bündelung" [bundling] by Alf Lechner

Mitte: „Haus der Liebe" von Norbert Tress
Rechts: „Öffnung" von Ingo Glass
Nächste Doppelseite:
„Piazza Verde" von Reiner Seliger

Centre: "Haus der Liebe" [house of love] by Norbert Tress
Right: "Öffnung" [opening] by Ingo Glass
Page 122/123: "Piazza Verde" by Reiner Seliger.

Links: „Figuren vor Block" von Michael Irmer
Mitte: „Innerer Konflikt" von Gianpietro Carlesso
Rechts: „Schatzkästchen" von Madeleine Dietz

Left: "Figures in front of block" by Michael Irmer
Centre: "Innerer Konflikt" [inner conflict] by Gianpietro Carlesso
Right: "Schatzkästchen" [treasure box] by Madeleine Dietz

Heil- und Würz-Kräuter

Schon Karl der Große erkannte die Kraft und Wirkung der Kräuter. Im »Capitulare de villis et curtis«, dem von ihm erlassenen Gesetz, wurde es Klöstern und Städten zur Pflicht gemacht, Nutzgärten anzulegen, in denen Kräuter zu Heil- und Würzzwecken kultiviert wurden.

Hier im Heilkräutergarten kann man rund 180 Kräuter betrachten – gegen jegliches Übel ist quasi ein Kräutlein gewachsen. Kräuterführungen laden ein in die spannende Welt von Digitalis und Co.

Medicinal and aromatic herbs

Even in his times, Charlemagne understood the power and effect of herbs. In the "Capitulare de villis et curtis" law he passed, cloisters and cities were made to plant kitchen gardens in which medicinal and aromatic herbs were to be cultivated.

The medicinal herb garden boasts around 180 herbs – there's a plant for practically every ailment. Herb guided tours give an insight into the fascinating world of digitalis and other plants.

KINDER

Für viele Mannheimer ist der Luisenpark Gartenersatz und Sommerwohnzimmer in einem. Das gilt insbesondere für die Kinder. Zahlreiche Spielplätze laden zum Spielen und Toben ein, „Wasser marsch" heißt es bei den Wasser-Spielplätzen, wo es sich auch herrlich „matschen" lässt. Auf der großen Freizeitwiese ist Platz zum Rennen und Ballspielen.

Das ganze Jahr über werden Aktionen und Projekte angeboten. Im Luisenpark ist immer etwas los, sommers wie winters.

CHILDREN

For many residents of Mannheim, the Luisenpark is both their substitute garden and summer living room in one. It's particularly true for children. Numerous playgrounds are the ideal place for fun and games, and in the water playgrounds they can jump in and get really muddy! The meadow provides plenty of space for running around and for ball games.

There are campaigns and projects the whole year round – there's always something going on at the Luisenpark, summer and winter.

„Schnullerbaum"
"Dummy tree"

Rasen betreten erwünscht - die Freizeitwiese
Please walk on the grass - the meadow

Der Burgspielplatz, Traum aller kleinen Ritter und Burgfräulein
The "castle playground" – what every small knight or damsel dreams of!

Der Bauernhof hat größte Anziehungskraft
The farmyard is the biggest attraction

Links: In der Fantasie fährt diese Lok wie der Blitz
Left: In the imagination, this train is as fast as lightning

Blick vom Wingert auf die Freizeitwiese
View from the vineyard over the meadow

Rangerkidz

Park-Ranger sind Jungs und Mädchen, die es genau wissen wollen - und das Wissen dann auch noch nutzbringend anwenden. Nach ihrer umfangreichen theoretischen und praktischen Schulung in der Grünen Schule und bei den Tierpflegern vor Ort, während der sie eine Menge über die verschiedenen Tiere im Park erfahren, über ihre Eigenheiten und Bedürfnisse, gehen sie „auf Streife" und haben ein wachsames Auge darauf, dass diese nicht gefüttert werden, weil ihnen das schadet. Und sie beantworten gerne Fragen und geben das Gelernte weiter.

Park rangers are boys and girls who are eager for knowledge – and want to put that knowledge to good use. After extensive theoretical and practical training in the "green school" and with the keepers in the park, during which they learn a great deal about the various animals in the park, their peculiarities and needs, they go "on the beat" and keep a close eye on making sure no-one feeds the animals, because it could do them harm. The children are also ready to answer questions and pass on what they have learned.

Wingert am Freizeithaus
Vineyard nearby Freizeithaus

Freizeitwiese im Herbst
Meadow in the autumn

Flamingos in Formation
Flamingos in formation

Otter und Humboldt-Pinguine
Otters and Humboldt penguins

Sattelstorch
Saddle-billed stork

Rastende Graugänse
Resting greylag geese

Enten-Kinderstube
The ducklings' nursery

Pelikan
Pelican

FEIERN IM PARK

Im Luisenpark ist gut feiern, kein Wunder beim schönsten Park der Kurpfalz, wo Kurpfälzer Lebensfreude auf herrliche Natur trifft. Im Sommer wie im Winter bieten sich viele Gelegenheiten und Örtlichkeiten an, sei es im privaten Rahmen wie Hochzeit oder runder Geburtstag oder im Großen beim Seebühnenzauber oder Ballonglühen.

FESTIVITIES IN THE PARK

The Luisenpark is an excellent place for a celebration – no wonder, in the most beautiful park in the Kurpfalz, where Kurpfalz joie de vivre and nature meet. In summer and winter, there are numerous opportunities and places to celebrate, be it a private ceremony such as a wedding or birthday, or on a larger scale at one of the Seebühnenzauber events or the hot air balloon glowing festival.

Ballonfestival

Röser

SWR 4 - Festival

SWR

Halloween

Am Ausklang des Sommermärchens steht Halloween. Nun wird es herbstlich im Park und der bunte Blütenflor durch die Pracht des bunten Laubes abgelöst.

Halloween

Halloween marks the end of the summer fairy tale. The park turns autumnal and the colourful blooms are replaced by the splendour of the colourful leaves.

Durchgehend geöffnet

Die orangeroten Papierkörbe fallen auf - besonders in einer weißen Winterlandschaft. Aber man sieht auch Fußspuren im Schnee - der Luisenpark ist nämlich durchgehend geöffnet. Mannheims grüne Oase lohnt selbst dann einen Ausflug, wenn sie ein weißes Kleid trägt. Ob im Frühling, wenn die Natur erst erwacht, oder im Herbst, wenn das Laub herrliche Farben annimmt, dann herabfällt und auf den Wegen knistert; stets ist der Park ein beliebtes Ausflugsziel. Da die rund 600 Liegen und Stühle witterungsbeständig sind und nie weggeräumt werden, kann man so auch goldene Oktobertage oder wunderbare Wintersonnenstrahlen genießen. Und sollte wirklich mal ein kalter Wind aufkommen, bietet sich zum Aufwärmen immer noch das Pflanzenschauhaus an. Die Park-Kassen sind bis Sonnenuntergang geöffnet, verlassen kann man den Park stets durch die Drehkreuze.

Always open

The orange rubbish bins stand out – particularly in a white winter landscape. But you can also see footprints in the snow – the Luisenpark is always open. Mannheim's green haven is even worth a visit when it's dressed in white. In spring, when nature is reawakening, or in autumn, when the leaves take on such wonderful colours and then fall and crunch under foot, the park is always a popular destination. As the 600 recliners and chairs are weather-resistant and are never cleared away, it's a wonderful place to enjoy a golden October day or the winter sun. And even if there is a cold gust of wind, the Plant House offers a warm sanctuary. The park cash desks are open until the sun goes down, and you can always exit the park through the rotating gates.

STIFTER & MÄZENE

Unzählige kleine und größere Spenden, Vermächtnisse und Zuwendungen für spezielle Projekte haben dazu beigetragen, den Park in seiner heutigen Gestalt zu schaffen.

Schon der Grundstock für den historischen Luisenpark war ein Vermächtnis in Höhe von 20.000 Goldmark, das Prof. Dr. C. Fuchs der Stadt Mannheim zweckgebunden für die Neuanlage eines Parks hinterlassen hatte.

Einer der größten „Anstifter" war Heinrich Vetter, heute ist es seine Stiftung. Nach ihm ist im Park sogar ein Weg benannt. Insgesamt 27 Kunstwerke bilden diese Einheit aus Kunst und Natur und sind an weiteren exponierten Stellen im Park zu finden. Auch zum Teehaus hat die Stiftung ihren Beitrag geleistet.

Das Erbe von Dipl. Kfm. Georg Schmuck bildete den Grundstock für den chinesischen Garten und das Teehaus, an dessen Verwirklichung der SAP-Gründer Klaus Tschira durch seine Stiftung nicht unerheblich beteiligt war.

Helene Heinrichs Erbe hat den Bau des Eulengeheges ermöglicht, die Anna-Maria-von-Schrader-Stiftung hat neben anderem das Aqua-Terrarium für die Anakondas sowie eine Quarantänestation für Tiere finanziert.

Ein beeindruckendes Beispiel für bürgerschaftliches Engagement ist der Förderverein Freunde des Luisenparks e.V. mit einigen Hundert Mitgliedern, dessen langjähriger Vorsitzender Ingo Kaltenborn gewesen war. Von Klettergerüst und Rollstuhlschaukel über Citrus- und Heilpflanzengarten bis Baumfarnhaus gäbe es heute viele Einrichtungen und Bauten des Parks ohne die Anregung und Finanzierung durch den Förderverein nicht.

PATRONS AND BENEFACTORS

Countless small and large donations, bequests and contributions for special projects have helped make the park what it is today.

The basis for the historical Luisenpark in the first place was a bequest of 20,000 gold marks, left to the city of Mannheim by Prof. Dr. C. Fuchs specifically for the creation of a new park.

One of the greatest benefactors was Heinrich Vetter; today it is his foundation. There is even a path named after him in the park. Twenty-seven works of art make up this amalgamation between art and nature and can also be found exhibited at further locations in the park. The foundation also contributed to the Teahouse.

The legacy of Dipl. Kfm. Georg Schmuck formed the basis for the Chinese Garden and Teahouse, and its creation was also funded to a considerable degree by SAP founder Klaus Tschira's foundation.

Helene Heinrich's legacy made it possible to build the owl enclosure, while the Anna-Maria-von-Schrader Foundation financed the aqua-terrarium for the anacondas, as well as an animal quarantine station.

One impressive example of citizen involvement is the association Freunde des Luisenparks e.V. [friends of the Luisenpark] with several hundred members, whose chairman of many years was Ingo Kaltenborn. Many of the facilities and buildings in the park, from the climbing frame and wheelchair swing, citrus and medicinal herb garden through to the Tree Fern House, would not exist today without association's input and financing.

Unser Dank gilt in besonderem Maße der Heinrich-Vetter-Stiftung, die auch die Entstehung dieses Buches unterstützt hat, sowie Herrn Jürgen Muley.

Our particular thanks go to the Heinrich Vetter Foundation, which also supported the production of this book, as well as to Mr. Jürgen Muley.

HEINRICH – VETTER – STIFTUNG